To Carolyn, Stuart, Jody, Skip, Vicken, and Bo for opening our eyes to ideas big and small —MB, MS, and ST

To Deb, for believing in me —TE

About This Book

The illustrations for this book were done in Procreate, using an iPad Pro and Apple Pencil. This book was edited by Samantha Gentry and designed by Brenda E. Angelilli.
The production was supervised by Bernadette Flinn, and the production editor was Jen Graham. The text was set in Brandon Text, and the display type is Dunkelbunt.

Little, Brown and Company
Hachette Book Group
1290 Avenue of the Americas, New York, NY 10104
Visit us at LBYR.com

First Edition: July 2023

Little, Brown and Company is a division of Hachette Book Group, Inc. The Little, Brown name and logo are trademarks of Hachette Book Group, Inc.

The publisher is not responsible for websites (or their content) that are not owned by the publisher.

Library of Congress Cataloging-in-Publication Data
Names: Bloom, Molly, 1983– author. | Sanchez, Marc, 1970– author. | Totten, Sanden, author. | Everett, Tiffany, 1990– illustrator.
Title: Brains on! presents…meet my micro-pets! / Molly Bloom, Marc Sanchez, and Sanden Totten ; illustrated by Tiffany Everett.
Other titles: Meet my micro-pets!
Description: First edition. | New York : Little, Brown and Company, 2023. | Audience: Ages 4–8 | Summary: "A fun and informative picture book all about the weird and wonderful community of tiny things living on and in our bodies!" —Provided by publisher.
Identifiers: LCCN 2022011873 | ISBN 9780316459471 (hardcover)
Subjects: LCSH: Microorganisms—Juvenile literature. | Human body—Microbiology—Juvenile literature.
Classification: LCC QR57 .B56 2023 | DDC 579—dc23/eng/20220509
LC record available at https://lccn.loc.gov/2022011873

ISBN 978-0-316-45947-1

PRINTED IN CHINA

APS

10 9 8 7 6 5 4 3 2 1

brains on! PRESENTS...

MEET MY MICRO-PETS!

MOLLY BLOOM, MARC SANCHEZ, and SANDEN TOTTEN

ILLUSTRATED by TIFFANY EVERETT

Little, Brown and Company

New York Boston

IT WAS SHOW-AND-TELL DAY in Ms. Abramson's third-grade class. Everyone loved show-and-tell day . . . especially Dominique.

Dominique knew that what she had to share was sensational! It was going to knock everyone's socks off, even the kids who were only wearing sandals.

She waited patiently as Ruthie shared her baseball mitt.

She tapped her foot while Leo shook his maracas.

She gave Didi's fuzzy dice a squeeze when they were passed around. And she agreed that Marcus's melted candy bar *did* look like George Washington, if you squinted.

At last, Ms. A turned to her and asked, "Dominique, what did you bring today?"

Dominique jumped to her feet, ran to the front of the class, and proudly said,  **"TA-DA!"**

Her classmates were confused.
Ms. A cleared her throat uncomfortably.
"Where's your show-and-tell?"
Aaliyah finally asked.

"You're looking at it!" Dominique declared. "Meet my micro-pets! They're more helpful than dogs, more beautiful than cats, cuddlier than gerbils, and way better than lizards. Sorry, Tisha."

Don't listen to her, Freddy.

"But I can't see anything," said Felix, who brought a pot holder he had crocheted. "You're doing a lot of telling and not a lot of showing."

"That's because they're too small to see with just your eyes," Dominique replied. "They're itsy-bitsy, teeny-tiny, little living things called microbes!

"I have one trillion micro-pets on me right now!" Dominique held out her arm. Her classmates squinted, but they still couldn't see anything.

"I've named each one! There's Jerry, Fuzzy, Polka Dot, Rachel, Celeste, Squirmy, Melinda, Archie, Snowball, Carlos, Rita, Bingo, Sticky, Harriet—"

"Uh, Dominique," Ms. A interrupted, "I'm not sure we have time to hear all their names. Why don't you tell us what your . . . um . . . micro-pets do?"

"Yeah!" said Tisha, holding her lizard tightly. "Freddy here can eat five crickets in one sitting!"

"The better question is, what *can't* my micro-pets do?

a world called a microbiome! I'm covered in bacteria . . .
you know, those living things made up of just one cell. I've also
got various viruses, funky families of fungi, and mini mites!

Her classmates looked shocked.

"Don't worry, they don't bite," Dominique said.

"But they do lay eggs on my skin!

"Their favorite spot is in my hair follicles—that's where the super-thin hairs on my face grow. I don't have to buy them pet food, because they just snack on the oils in my skin and also bacteria and dead skin cells. How's that for a mite-y meal?!

"They've been living on humans for so long that the DNA from face mites can give clues about where a person's ancestors lived long, long ago."

Lulu raised her hand. "Okay, I'll admit those mites sound pretty cool. But aren't bacteria and viruses and the other stuff bad for you? I had a cold virus last week, and it was no fun!"

"Sure, some microbes are bad and can make you sick," Dominique replied. "But *my* micro-pets are pretty much harmless, and some are even helpful!

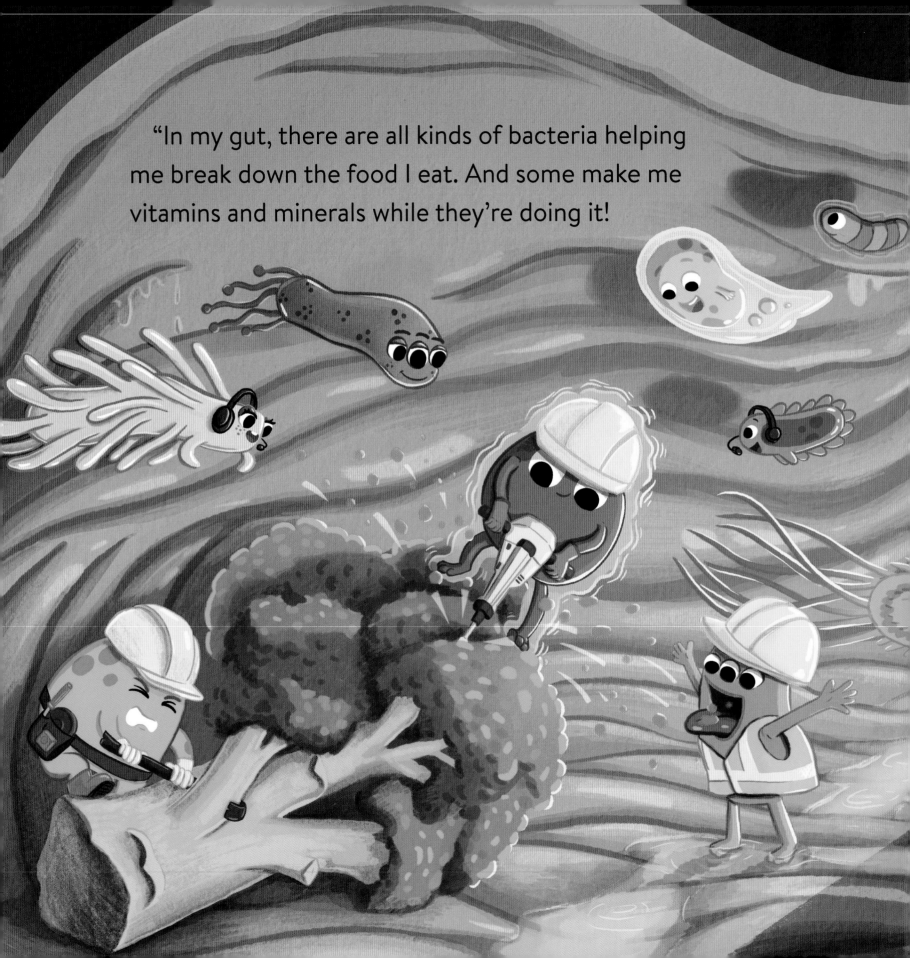

"In my gut, there are all kinds of bacteria helping me break down the food I eat. And some make me vitamins and minerals while they're doing it!

"And speaking of happiness, who here smiles when they hear a fart?"

Hands shot up. The class erupted in laughter. Ms. A held her nose.

"My micro-pets are a fart factory! They make gas when they eat and it fills up my insides. Then, when there's enough gas—*kaboom!* Mega-fart! So when I toot, it's all thanks to my micro-pets.

"The micro-pets on my skin are also great guards," Dominique added.

"Like my goldendoodle Ella?" Coco asked. "She guards the yard from squirrels."

"Exactly like Ella," Dominique replied. "My micro-pets fight off bad bacteria, block nasty germs, and even help keep my skin cells strong and healthy.

"My mouth microbes help eat the food stuck between my teeth, and then they turn it all into cool plaque sculptures! They're like nonstop artists!

"I make sure to brush and floss so it doesn't get too crowded in here with their work.

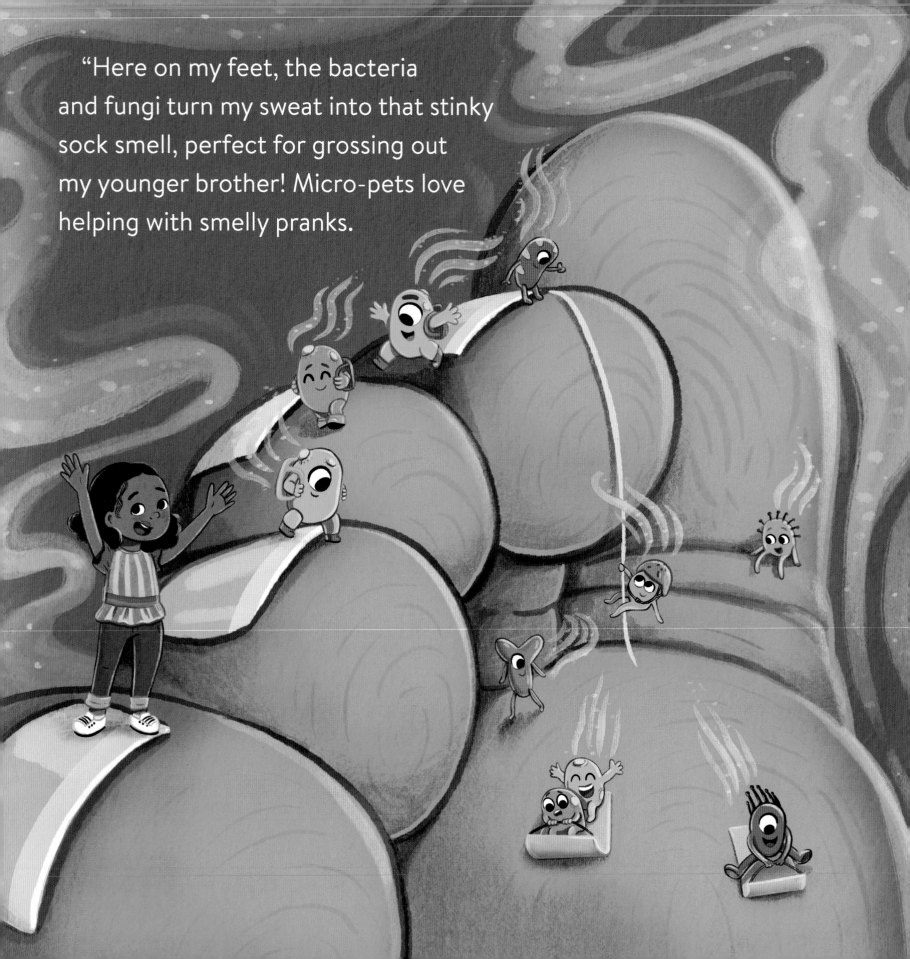

"Here on my feet, the bacteria and fungi turn my sweat into that stinky sock smell, perfect for grossing out my younger brother! Micro-pets love helping with smelly pranks.

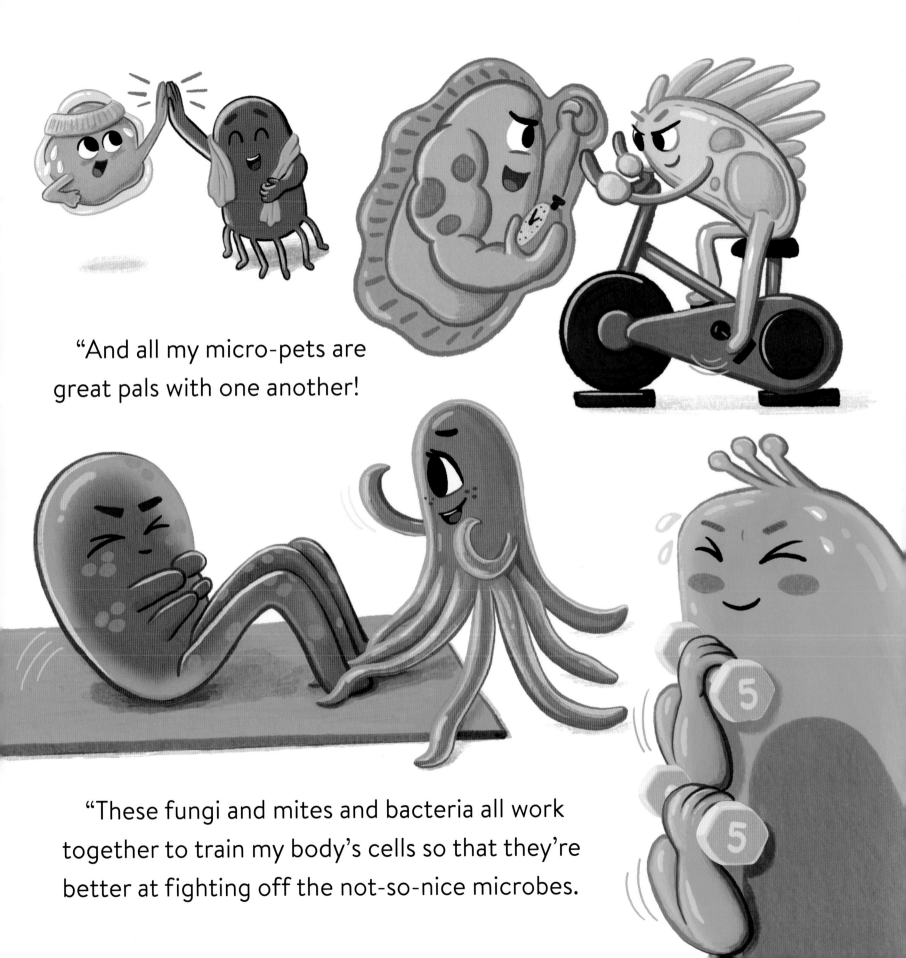

"And all my micro-pets are great pals with one another!

"These fungi and mites and bacteria all work together to train my body's cells so that they're better at fighting off the not-so-nice microbes.

"But mostly my microbes just keep me company! Plus, they're great listeners, they love to snuggle, and I never need to walk them. My micro-pets are truly perfect pals."

"I want micro-pets!" exclaimed Tisha.

The rest of the class joined in. "Me too! Me too!"

Dominique gave a big smile. "Well, guess what? You already have them!"

The class gasped.

"All humans do. So take good care of your micro-pets, because they help take care of you. Oh, and don't forget to name each and every one!"

WHAT IS A MICROBIOME?

Your microbiome is made up of the microbes—teeny organisms that you can't see with just your eyes (you'd need a microscope)—that live in and on your body. Your body contains ten times more microbes than it does cells. Which means you have *trillions* of micro-pets!

But no need to get icked out—these microbes are super friendly and important to your health. The idea of studying your microbiome is fairly new, so scientists are learning more all the time about what our microbiome does for us.

Each person's microbiome has a unique makeup, but get this: Scientists have found that people who live together tend to have similar microbiomes. Not only do you share the bathroom with the people in your house—you share microbes too!

MEET YOUR MICROBIOME!

BACTERIA: These microscopic living things are made up of just a single cell. There are many, many different kinds of bacteria. Some can make pretty stinky odors, like those from your feet, armpits, and farts!

MITES: These tiny eight-legged arthropods are closely related to ticks and spiders. They feed off the oil your skin makes and spend their entire life on you! Since mites and humans have been living together for a long time, scientists can learn about your ancestors by looking at the DNA of your mites.

VIRUSES: Viruses are not really alive, because they need other creatures' cells in order to make more copies of themselves. The viruses in our microbiome help keep our bacteria in check so there aren't too many of them. It's all about balance!

FUNGI: These organisms come in many shapes and sizes. They digest their food externally, or outside their bodies. That means they break down the matter around them and then absorb the nutrients. It seems the fungi in our gut microbiome help train our immune system and make it stronger.

TAKING YOUR MICRO-PETS FOR A WALK

Our microbiome isn't just *on* us—it's also all around us. Scientists have discovered that there is an invisible cloud of bacteria, fungi, and dead skin cells floating outside each and every one of us. Every time we move, we send microbes flying off our skin. These critters then get on the furniture, walls, and people nearby, even if we never touch them.

MOMENT OF UM: MICROBIOME EDITION

WHY DO FARTS SMELL?

ANSWER: The bacteria in your intestines that help break down your food create gas in the process. This gas comes out of you as farts! Depending on what you eat, the gas will have different smells. Broccoli, for instance, contains sulfur, so the bacteria produce hydrogen sulfide, which has an egglike odor.

WHY DO ADULTS HAVE STINKY ARMPITS BUT KIDS USUALLY DON'T?

ANSWER: There are two different kinds of sweat glands in your armpits. One is called an eccrine sweat gland, and its main job is to keep you cool. The other is the apocrine sweat gland, and it makes sweat when you're stressed out. This is the kind of sweat that is eaten by bacteria that make a stinky gas. These apocrine glands don't make sweat until your body starts changing from a kid's body into a grown-up one.

LISTEN ON!

You can learn more about your microbiome from these episodes of the *Brains On!* podcast:

- **Poop party: Answers to your poo questions** (August 11, 2020)
- **The secret world of dust** (February 25, 2020)
- **Thinkin' stinkin': Why we smell** (April 30, 2019)
- **Science under the microscope** (October 9, 2018)
- **Fart smarts: Understanding the gas we pass** (July 4, 2017)